HANDMADE CANDLES
& Smudge Sticks

HANDMADE CANDLES
& Smudge Sticks

35 inspiring step-by-step projects

EMMA HARDY

Photography by **Debbie Patterson**

CICO BOOKS
LONDON NEW YORK

Published in 2019 by CICO Books
An imprint of Ryland Peters & Small Ltd
20–21 Jockey's Fields   341 E 116th St
London WC1R 4BW   New York, NY 10029

www.rylandpeters.com

10 9 8 7 6 5 4 3 2 1

A CIP catalog record for this book is available from
the Library of Congress and the British Library.

ISBN: 978-1-78249-751-6

Printed in China

Photographer: Debbie Patterson
Stylist: Emma Hardy

Editor: Anna Galkina
Art director: Sally Powell
Production controller: David Hearn
Publishing manager: Penny Craig
Publisher: Cindy Richards

Contents

Introduction

If you are keen to start making candles and smudge sticks, this book of 35 projects is the perfect introduction. While there is a huge variety of store-bought candles available these days, making your own is infinitely more satisfying—and a lot cheaper, too.

Starting with a chapter on smudge sticks, which are increasingly popular and surprisingly easy to make, there are then five chapters on candle-making, providing you with all the instructions you need to get started. From using plastic, metal, and rubber molds, to dipping, making container candles, and adding scents, the projects will guide you from start to finish so you can create a wide range of handmade designs.

The basic process of candle-making is a simple one, but perfecting scent throws, dyeing wax, and fine-tuning the finish of a candle can be quite a science. It is worth reading the techniques and materials section (see pages 8–12), which explains the basics. Inevitably, there will be some mistakes and unexpected results because a number of factors will influence the success of your candles, but experimentation is all part of the fun. Have a look at page 13 for some easy fixes for common errors that candle-makers may encounter. With all this in mind, try not to get too hung up on technical details—let your creativity guide the way.

There are lots of different waxes and wicks available, offering different qualities and characteristics. I recommend starting with a basic paraffin or soy wax and simple pre-primed wicks, and as you become more accomplished, you may wish to try out different waxes, dyes, and scents to achieve different effects.

If you are making a large batch of candles it is wise to pour one of them, check the wick size, color, or fragrance, amend it if necessary, then make the rest, so that you do not end up with lots of candles that you are unhappy with.

And lastly, it's a good idea to keep a notebook with details of the fragrance and dye quantities and wax temperatures you have used for each project, so that you can learn from your experiences. It is very useful to be able to look back on previous candle projects that have worked well.

This book will hopefully equip you with all the skills and expertise you need to not only make these projects, but to go on to create your own candles and smudge sticks and personalize the designs with your own style.

Smudge sticks

A smudge stick is a bundle of herbs that has been dried and can be burned for its cleansing and purifying properties. Burning herbs in this way is an ancient ritual used by the indigenous people of North America. It's now popular with New Age healers and many other cultures around the world. Traditionally, smudge sticks are made using specific herbs and plants that are harvested at particular times for their individual qualities. They are bundled up, left to dry, then burned in a ceremonial way called "smudging" to help remove negative energy and restore balance. The smudge sticks in this book do not pretend to be authentic, but they can help to bring the outdoors in and create a calm atmosphere in your home. They allow you to use the basic premise of smudging in a simple and easy way. Below are some of the most commonly used herbs for smudge sticks—feel free to pick your own based on scent and accessibility.

WHITE SAGE—thought to help dispel negativity and is ideal for cleansing the home. Culinary sage can also be burned, but some people find its smell overpowering.

CEDAR—thought to attract good spirits, useful for cleansing a new home and eliminating negative energies.

LAVENDER—believed to have protective powers, brings positive energy, and promotes love.

ROSEMARY—can help to ward off evil spirits, reduce nightmares, and can bring clarity.

MUGWORT—thought to promote physical wellbeing and can help to improve endurance.

JUNIPER—believed to have invigorating qualities and can stimulate the mind, body, and spirit, as well as imparting a beautiful scent.

PINE—can be used for its cleansing and purifying qualities.

ROSE PETALS AND BLOOMS—can create a meditative and calm atmosphere, and a lingering delicate scent.

EUCALYPTUS—has a cleansing scent and is useful for health and healing.

THYME—thought to encourage positivity and courage.

LEMON BALM—can bring spiritual cleansing and useful for restoring calm.

Smudge sticks need to be left to dry for at least two weeks before lighting. To use them, light the end, then blow the flame out. Place the smudge stick on a heatproof dish or plate and leave to smoke or, holding the unlit end, wave the smudge stick slowly around the room so that the smoke spreads. A couple of minutes of smudging should be enough —you can leave it to burn out on a heatproof dish. If left to burn for too long, smudge sticks will produce a lot of smoke. Open a window if necessary. If it continues to smoke, gently rub it over a heatproof surface to extinguish it. A smudge stick can be used several times, although do not light it too close to the end of the stick as it will not be safe to handle.

important safety information

Never leave smoking smudge sticks unattended.
Ensure that they are completely extinguished before storing them.
Make sure that they are never left on a surface that may become damaged by heat.
Do not smudge directly around children and animals.

Candles

Candles are available in a huge range of shapes, sizes, and scents. This makes candle-making an exciting process as there are so many variations. Here are the basic candle shapes:

PILLAR CANDLES—these are single candles, usually cylindrical in shape. They are made in simple molds and can be made in a huge range of colors. They are usually made from paraffin wax with added stearin—this creates a hard finish and does not drip too much when lit.

DIPPED CANDLES—these are the oldest and most traditional type of candle, made by repeatedly dipping wicks into molten wax. They do not require a mold, but need a deep dipping can to hold the wax. They can be made from both paraffin wax and beeswax. They can be left plain for a simple, classic look or twisted and embellished for a more interesting finish.

CONTAINER CANDLES—cans, glasses, jars, and anything else that is watertight can all be used to make container candles. Often scented, container candles are very easy to make and are ideal if you want to make several candles at the same time. Beeswax and paraffin wax can be used, but will need to be topped up as the wax will usually dip while hardening. Soy wax can also be used; it has a lovely creamy color, scent and dyes can be added easily, and it tends not to dip in the middle when hardening.

MOLDED CANDLES—these can be made in a huge variety of shapes using store-bought rubber, glass, plastic, and metal molds. Paraffin wax is perfect for this type of candle as it is hard and will keep its shape well. Beeswax can also be used but can be tricky to remove from molds as it is quite sticky.

Materials

WAXES

The following information about waxes will give you a general guide, but there are many different paraffin, beeswax, and soy waxes available so always take note of information supplied when buying the product for specific details, as factors such as melting points can vary.

PARAFFIN
This wax is a good, all-round wax that is colorless, odorless, and suitable for making a wide range of candles. It is a by-product of the oil-refining industry and usually comes in pellet form, but can be bought in bricks, too. A basic paraffin wax can be used for pillar candles made in molds, dipped candles, or container candles. There are many different paraffin waxes for candle-making available—those with higher melting points (above 130°F/54°C) are suitable for pillar candles as the wax will be hard and hold its shape well. Lower melting-point paraffin wax can be used for container candles. Candles made from paraffin wax will dip and need topping up as they harden. Some paraffin waxes have stearin already added (see Stearin, right), so check when buying.

SOY
This wax is derived from soy beans and is more eco-friendly than paraffin wax, as it is completely renewable and

biodegradable. It is available in pellets and flakes. It is suitable for container candles and has a lovely, creamy color, with a cleaner burn than paraffin wax, producing less soot. Its scent throw (see Vybar, below) is not as strong as paraffin wax and it requires more dye to create stronger colors, but it does not require topping up when cooling, and its pouring temperatures are less important than for paraffin wax.

BEESWAX
This is a completely natural wax that is available in white or yellow pellets or bricks. It is also sold in sheets which can be bought in a range of colors. It burns slower, cleaner, and with a brighter flame than other waxes, making it a beautiful wax for candle-making. It is, however, very expensive compared to other waxes, and has a sticky quality which makes it tricky to work with, especially when using molds. Beeswax should not be used for vegan-friendly candles—soy wax is a good alternative as it is plant-based and sustainable.

STEARIN
Stearin helps wax to shrink, making it easier to remove candles from their molds. It can give a better depth of color, with a harder finish. It can also reduce dripping and give candles a slower burning time. It should be used one part stearin to 10 parts wax, so 7oz (200g) of wax will require ¾oz (20g) of stearin. Sometimes paraffin wax can be bought with added stearin, but if your wax does not have stearin, it is worth adding it yourself, especially if making candles in plastic or metal molds. It should not be used in rubber molds as it can cause the rubber to disintegrate. Stearin is not vegan as it is derived from animal fat. Coconut- and palm-based stearins are available to buy from specialist candle-making suppliers, they are a little more expensive but are 100% vegan.

VYBAR
Vybar is a polymer that can be used to increase the scent throw of candles. When added to wax, it can create a harder finish and will make candles more opaque. It can be used instead of stearin if using rubber molds to help with candle release. I use 5% vybar to wax (or one

Clockwise from top: beeswax, paraffin wax, stearin, and soy wax

part vybar to 20 parts wax) so 7oz (200g) of wax will require ⅓oz (10g) of vybar. Using too much vybar can actually prevent scent throw, so do not add more than this. While it is not essential in candle-making, it can be a useful additive and can be worth using if you would like to make strongly-scented candles.

Cotton and linen wicks

Wick sustainers and ready-made wicks

WICKS

It is important to use the correct wick when making candles. A wick that is too small will prevent the candle burning properly and may cause the candle to extinguish prematurely. Too large a wick will cause the candle to flare and produce a lot of soot. Wicks are usually made from cotton, but often have linen, paper, or zinc (for increased burning times) added to them. They are sold in different sizes, from ½in (1cm) to 4in (10cm). Try to buy wick that has been pre-primed (dipped in wax), as this will burn better. The diameter of your candle will dictate the wick required. As a basic guide, a candle with a diameter of 1in (2.5cm) will require a 1-in (2.5-cm) wick. There are many wicks offering specific qualities available to buy, so check when buying to make sure you are purchasing the correct wick for each project to ensure successful candle-making. Wicks can be bought pre-fitted with sustainers (holders) or sold separately.

WICK SUSTAINERS (HOLDERS)

These are small metal circles for adding to the bottom of your wicks. Once a wick is threaded through the hole in the center, the fitting can be tightened using small pliers to hold the wick. Wick sustainers enable the candle to continue burning right to the end without the wick falling over.

WAX ADHESIVE

This is available in a solid bar or as patches (often called "glue dots") to be used to stick wick sustainers to the bottom of containers. Wax adhesive in bars can also be melted in a double boiler and painted onto candles to stick decorations like leaves and dried flowers onto them.

MOLD SEAL

This is a putty-like substance that is used around wicks and molds to seal them and prevent wax leaking out. It is reuseable if kept clean and dust-free.

SCENTS AND OILS

Scents made specifically for candle-making are widely available and come in a huge range of aromas. Often, they are mixtures of natural essential oils and synthetic compounds. Pure essential oils can be used, but the temperature of the molten wax should be dropped slightly before adding them, or the essential oil may evaporate away slightly, reducing the strength of the scent. Check before using them, as some give off unpleasant smells when burned. Specialist candle scents are less troublesome to use as they are made for the job, and are often available without too many synthetic additives, plus they are often vegan.

DYES

Wax dye can be bought in liquid, powder, and disc form. It is available in a wide selection of colors which can be mixed together to form many shades. It is a good idea to buy a basic set of dyes in red, blue, yellow, black, cream, brown, green, and pink, which will allow you to make a wide range of colors.

Equipment

BASIC CANDLE-MAKING KIT

DOUBLE BOILER

It is very important not to heat wax directly over a flame or heat source, so a double boiler is essential when candle-making. A bowl can be placed over a pan of water to melt wax, but a double boiler (they can often be bought cheaply online or from catering equipment stores) will be safer and much easier to use. The bottom pan should be half-full of boiling water to melt wax in the top pan (filling it all the way can cause the water to splutter out of the pan, which should be avoided so that water does not reach the melting wax). Check the water level regularly when using to make sure that the pan does not boil dry. After using the double boiler, pour any excess wax out, empty the water from the bottom, wipe both pans with paper towels, and leave to dry completely.

THERMOMETER

Candle-making requires wax to be melted to specific temperatures to achieve the best finishes, so a thermometer is essential. Specialist candle-making thermometers are available to buy, but kitchen thermometers can be also used as long as their upper range can reach 350°F (177°C). After use wipe it clean with a paper towel and store in its box to prevent damage.

WOODEN SPOON

Used to mix waxes and dyes. Do not use your candle-making spoon in food preparation.

PITCHER (JUG)

A cheap plastic one will work well. Particularly useful for pouring waxes into small containers and molds, and essential if your double boiler does not have a lip for pouring.

OTHER USEFUL EQUIPMENT

DIPPING CAN

This is essential for making dipped candles. Available from candle-making supply stores, it is a deep metal can for melting wax that can be used in a pan of simmering water. Dipping cans require a lot of wax to fill them, so check when buying. Always wipe excess wax from the inside of the can after use and dry the outside well. Alternatively, large catering cans could also be used to dip. Ensure that they are thoroughly clean and dry before using.

MOLDS

Candle moulds are available in glass, plastic, rubber, and metal and come in a huge range of shapes and sizes. Most molds can be used multiple times if looked after properly. Always clean them after use. If using rubber molds and paraffin wax, make sure the wax does not contain added stearin, as this could damage the rubber.

CONTAINERS

There are endless possibilities for being creative with containers. Metal, glass, and ceramic containers can all be used as long as they are watertight.

WICKING NEEDLE

These are long metal needles that are very strong and inflexible. They are useful when using rubber molds as they allow you to thread wicks through the molds. They can also be used to hold wicks in place across the base of a candle.

OTHER HANDY TOOLS

- Scissors—for cutting and trimming wicks
- Small pliers—needed to fix wick sustainers onto wicks
- Paper towels
- Old newspaper—to protect surfaces
- Old, clean plastic food boxes (from take-out meals) are perfect for storing excess molten wax
- Wooden skewers and dolly pins (clothes pegs)—useful for holding wicks in place
- Old white saucer or plate to drip wax on if using dyes—you can see an example of the color you have mixed

Adding and mixing dye into melted wax

bear in mind that these drips of wax will be much less concentrated than the final candle.

ADDING SCENT

As a general rule, 5–10% fragrance should be used, so for 1lb (500g) wax, use 5% scent (¾oz/25g) initially, adding up to 10% (1¾oz/50g) if you would like a stronger fragrance. Bear in mind that most waxes have a maximum scent load and scents may not become any stronger despite more oils being added. The quantities needed will vary depending on the fragrances and waxes that you use, so experiment until you are happy with the results.

USING MOLDS

To clean metal molds, place them in an oven on a low heat until the wax has melted, remove from the oven wearing oven mitts, and wipe the molds clean with paper towels. For glass, plastic, and rubber molds, place the molds in a sink of hot, soapy water and, wearing rubber gloves, wipe the molds clean with a cloth. Dry them thoroughly before storing.

STORING AND BURNING CANDLES

There are a few tips when burning candles that will help to get the best out of your handmade candles:

- Keep candles out of direct sunlight to prevent them melting and their colors bleaching. Store them in a cool, dry, and dust-free place.
- Trim the wick to ⅛in (3mm) before lighting.
- Wax has a memory, so it is important to melt the candle adequately on the first burn to prevent tunneling, memory rings (see page 13), and uneven burning in future. When lighting a candle for the first time, allow it to burn for one hour for every 1in (2.5cm) in diameter of the actual candle size.
- Always keep lit candles out of drafts. This will prevent anything nearby from setting alight and will allow the candle to burn evenly.
- To extinguish a candle, push the wick into the molten wax slightly or use a candle snuffer. This will make it easier to relight next time you use it.

Techniques

WORKING OUT WAX QUANTITIES

Before you start melting any wax, you will need to work out how much wax you will need for each mold or container. To do this, fill the mold or container with water (blocking any holes with mold seal) and pour the water into a measuring pitcher (jug). Round up the amount of water to the nearest ⅓oz (10ml). For every 3⅓oz (100ml) water, you will need 3oz (90g) wax. Ensure that the mold or container is thoroughly dry before filling it with molten wax. Melting too much wax is not a problem, as any excess can be poured into a spare plastic box and stored for later use.

MELTING WAX

Wax should always be melted in a double boiler and never directly over a flame or heat source. It can take a while for wax to melt, especially if you are using large quantities, but never be tempted to leave your double boiler whilst melting wax, as the temperature of the wax can increase quickly and the wax can easily reach its flash point (where it may burst into flames). Check melting wax regularly with a thermometer. If your dry wax will not fit in the double boiler, melt some of it, and then add more wax to it gradually to melt all of it. You can stir the wax gently to mix in dye and scent, but try not to stir

too vigorously as that may cause air bubbles to form and create an uneven finish on the candle.

TEMPERATURES

Wax needs to be melted to certain temperatures when making candles. Once wax has reached its required temperature, take it off the heat. Some of the projects in this book require the wax to cool a little before pouring (for example, when adding scents and dipping) and this will take a little experimentation on your part. It does not take long for wax to cool. Paraffin wax—heat to 180°F (80°C) before pouring. Soy wax—heat to 140°F (60°C) before pouring. Beeswax—heat to 140°F (60°C) before pouring.

ADDING DYE

Wax dyes are easy to use, but obtaining the color you want can be a little tricky. Follow the manufacturer's instructions as a basic guide, but trial and error can be the only way, starting off with small amounts of dye and erring on the side of caution (whether you are using liquid, powder, or discs). Add dye to your wax and ensure it has completely mixed in, drip a little wax onto a white saucer or plate and leave for a few seconds to harden. This will help you to gauge whether more dye is needed, although

Troubleshooting

Candle-making is a lot of fun, but mistakes and problems are inevitable when starting out. Don't let this put you off. Here are a few common problems that you may encounter, with solutions to help.

TUNNELING AND MEMORY RINGS

This can be caused by a wick that is too small. It causes the wax to melt unevenly or in a small circle around the wick, and can also affect the scent throw of a candle. Increase the size of the wick when making more candles. Wax has a memory and will only burn to its original burning point, so ensure that when you first burn a candle it melts across the whole candle before extinguishing it, so that it will burn effectively when lit again.

MUSHROOMING

If a candle produces lots of soot and burns with a large flame, it may be mushrooming. This is caused by a wick that is too large or it can sometimes be caused by using too much scent. Try smaller wicks or reduce the amount of scent added to the molten wax.

DIPPING

Paraffin wax naturally dips in the middle and can be topped up in molds and containers as it hardens. If your soy wax dips around the wick, try pouring it at a lower temperature. Let the candle set at an even room temperature.

CRACKED SURFACE

Cracks in the surface of the wax can be caused by water in the mold. Make sure that molds are completely dry before using.

FROSTING

Sometimes small, white frost marks appear on the surface of the candle. This is caused by oils in the wax crystalizing. Try to reduce the pouring temperature to prevent frosting and keep the room temperature even, making sure that it is not too hot or too cold.

SWEATING

Droplets forming on the top of the candle can be caused by using too much scent. Reduce the amount of fragrance.

WAX PULLS AWAY FROM THE CONTAINER

This can be caused by wax being too cool when poured. Check the temperature of the wax before pouring. It can also be caused by wax cooling too quickly. Leave the candles to set at room temperature.

COLOR NOT AS EXPECTED

Adding dyes can be trial and error. It can be disheartening to see that candles are not the color you wanted when set, but if they are truly not right, simply remelt them and add more dye to strengthen the color, or use a small piece of the candle and more wax to dilute the color a little. With experience, using dyes will get easier. Make a note of how much dye is used in each batch for future reference.

CANDLE DIFFICULT TO REMOVE FROM ITS MOLD

Put the candle in the fridge for about half an hour. This will cause the wax to shrink a little so that the candle will easily pull away from the mold.

LOW SCENT THROW

There can be several reasons for this:
- Not enough scent was used when making the candle: increase the scent for future candles.
- The scent was added when the wax was too hot and so has evaporated: cool the wax slightly before adding scent.

- The scent was not mixed adequately into the wax when melting: Stir slowly and gently to ensure that it has dispersed completely before pouring.

SPUTTERING FLAME

This can be caused by water in the wax or air pockets in the wax. Keep water away from the wax when melting and pouring and ensure that molds are completely dry. Do not stir the wax too vigorously when melting to prevent air bubbles forming.

CANDLE BURNING TOO QUICKLY

This can be caused by air pockets in the wax or low-quality wax. Try not to stir the molten wax too vigorously when melting, and experiment with alternative waxes.

CHAPTER 1 SMUDGE *sticks*

WHITE SAGE *smudge sticks*

Sage is considered to be useful for reducing negativity and can be used to cleanse the home. Choose stems with large leaves to make it easier to create a tight bundle.

TOOLS & MATERIALS

White sage, several bunches

Cotton thread

Scissors

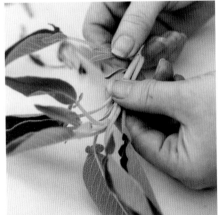

1 Pick any small leaves from the sage using your fingertips.

2 Gather several bunches (three or four, although this will depend on the size available to you). Tie the thread around the bottom, finishing with a knot, leaving the end of the thread long enough to tie a final knot in Step 7.

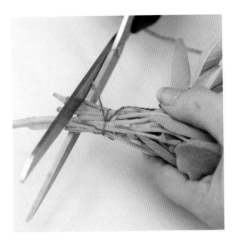

3 Trim the stems neatly with scissors.

4 Wrap the thread upward around the bundle, pulling it firmly but not hard enough to damage the sage leaves.

5 Wrap the thread around the top of the bundle a few times, again pulling it firmly.

6 Work down the bundle with the thread, making an even criss-cross pattern.

7 Tie the end of the thread to the end of the initial knot and trim the ends of the thread neatly.

8 Trim the top and bottom of the smudge stick with a straight cut at both ends. Leave the smudge stick somewhere warm and dry for at least two weeks before lighting.

ROSEMARY *smudge sticks*

Rosemary is traditionally used to ward off evil spirits and help banish nightmares. Use it for its cleansing properties and to bring clarity. Make sure you leave the smudge sticks to dry out for a couple of weeks before burning.

TOOLS & MATERIALS

Sprigs of fresh rosemary

Cotton cord

Scissors

1 Gather rosemary sprigs of similar length in your hand. Sprigs of differing lengths will be more difficult to tie into a neat bundle.

2 Tie cord around the base of the bundle, finishing with a knot, leaving the end of the cord long enough to tie a final knot in Step 6.

3 Squeeze the bundle in the palm of your hand firmly. This will flatten the needles of the rosemary and make a neater, more compact smudge stick.

4 Wrap the cord diagonally around the bundle, trying to catch needles that are sticking out under the cord. Pull the cord firmly.

5 Wind the cord around the top of the bundle a few times, pulling it firmly.

6 Wrap the cord back down the bundle, criss-crossing it neatly and again trying to flatten any needles that are sticking out, pulling the cord tightly. Finish with a secure knot at the bottom and trim the cord.

7 Trim the bottom and top of the smudge stick neatly with scissors and leave somewhere warm and dry for at least two weeks before lighting.

MUGWORT *smudge stick*

Mugwort (artemisia) is used to promote physical wellbeing and improve endurance. It has feathery leaves so you will need several branches of it to make a bundle—squeeze the leaves as you tie it so that it becomes compact and solid.

TOOLS & MATERIALS

Mugwort plant

Pruning shears (secateurs)

Colored raffia

1 Cut branches from the mugwort plant using pruning shears (secateurs), leaving about 4in (10cm) of leafless branch on each one. Remove any small or dead leaves from the bottom of the branches with your fingertips.

2 Bundle the branches together, holding the ends firmly between your fingers, and tie raffia firmly around the base so that they are securely held together. Leave the end of the raffia long enough to tie a final knot in Step 6.

3 Squeezing the bundle as you go to compress the leaves, wrap the raffia diagonally around the bundle, pulling it firmly.

4 Neatly wrap the raffia around the top of the bundle several times.

5 Wrap the raffia back down to the base of the bundle, catching any stray bits of leaf that are sticking out.

6 Tie the raffia in a knot at the base and trim neatly. Trim the bottom of the branches with one neat cut using pruning shears (secateurs). Trim the top of the smudge stick in the same way to neaten it. Leave somewhere warm and dry for at least two weeks before lighting.

JUNIPER *smudge stick*

Used for its reviving and stimulating qualities, juniper aids the mind, body, and spirit. Stems of juniper can be quite long but you don't have to burn the whole smudge stick at once —simply put out the burning end to save it for another time.

TOOLS & MATERIALS

Long lengths of juniper branches

Pruning shears (secateurs)

Natural twine

1 Cut stems of juniper to the same length using pruning shears (secateurs). Tie the ends together securely with twine, finishing with a knot. Leave enough twine to tie a final knot in Step 5.

2 Squeeze the branches together (if your juniper is particularly spiky you may need to wear gardening gloves for this) and wrap the twine around the bundle horizontally, trying to catch any needles that stick out under the twine and pulling the twine firmly.

3 Bind the twine around the top of the bundle, wrapping it firmly around the juniper several times.

4 Wrap the twine back down the bundle in a criss-cross pattern. Again, pull the twine firmly.

5 Tie the twine in a secure knot at the bottom and trim the ends of the twine neatly.

6 Trim the bottom of the smudge stick with one neat snip using the pruning shears (secateurs).

7 Trim the top in the same way to neaten it. Leave the finished smudge stick somewhere warm and dry for at least two weeks before lighting.

TOOLS & MATERIALS

White sage, several bunches

Lavender sprigs

Cotton thread

Scissors

LAVENDER AND SAGE *smudge sticks*

Lavender has long been used for its relaxing qualities and teaming it with sage will bring calm and peace to a room. Use this smudge stick to dispel stress, to encourage restfulness, to restore balance—or simply enjoy it for its lovely aroma.

1 Take a few bunches of sage and remove any small leaves using your fingertips. Gather the bunches together by holding their bases.

2 Take some sprigs of lavender and wrap them round the sage bundle so that they are evenly spread around the sage. Tie cotton thread around the base and finish with a tight knot, leaving the end of the thread long enough to tie a final knot in Step 6.

3 Start to wrap the thread around the bundle, pulling it firmly but not hard enough to damage the sage leaves.

4 Wrap the thread around the top of the smudge stick a few times, again pulling the thread firmly but not enough to damage the leaves.

5 Wrap the thread back down the smudge stick in a criss-cross pattern, keeping the thread taut.

6 Finish by tying the ends of the thread together at the base of the smudge stick. Trim the ends of the thread.

7 Trim the base and the top of the smudge stick and leave somewhere warm and dry for at least two weeks before lighting.

FLOWER *smudge sticks*

These smudge sticks look so pretty and would make a great gift. Eucalyptus has purifying properties and can encourage good health and healing, thyme brings positivity and courage, and fresh flowers offer a visual treat.

TOOLS & MATERIALS

Thyme sprigs

Eucalyptus stems

Stalks of flowering plants (chamomile, mimosa, or any other small-scale flowers)

Scissors

Natural twine

1 Gather some sprigs of thyme in your hand and hold their bases firmly.

2 Cut a few stems of eucalyptus and stalks of flowers to the same length and bundle them around the thyme.

4 Wrap the twine round the bundle, tucking leaves and flowers under the twine as you go.

5 Wrap the twine around the top of the bundle several times.

3 Tie the twine round the bottom and fasten with a secure knot. Leave the end of the twine long enough to tie a final knot in Step 7. Make sure that the twine is pulled tightly to secure all the stems.

6 Continue to wrap the twine around the bundle, working from the top down in a criss-cross pattern. Pull it firmly as you go.

7 Fasten with a secure knot at the bottom and trim the twine.

8 Using scissors, snip the top and the bottom of the bundle to make a neat edge. Leave somewhere warm and dry for at least two weeks before lighting.

CHAPTER 2 CANDLES
in containers

MATERIALS

Wick

Wick sustainer

Wax adhesive

Large shell

Paper towels

Soy wax

TOOLS

Basic candle-making kit (see page 11)

Small pliers

Wooden skewer

Bowl—larger than the shell

SHELL *candles*

Choose larger shells with a wide opening so that they can be filled with plenty of wax. Make sure that they can sit level when lit so that the surface of the wax is horizontal, otherwise the candle will not burn evenly and wax may pour out when molten.

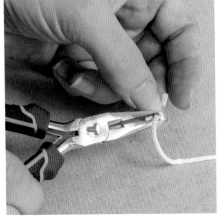

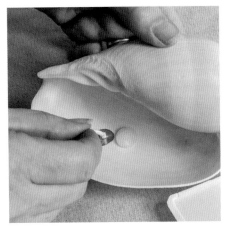

1 Cut a length of wick about 2in (5cm) longer than you need the final wick to be. Push the end of the wick into the wick sustainer and fix in place with the pliers.

2 Dot a small piece of wax adhesive inside the shell and stick the bottom of the wick sustainer onto it, pushing it down gently so it is firmly held in place.

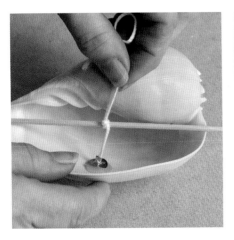

3 Cut a piece of wooden skewer so that it can rest across the shell. Tie the wick onto it with a loose knot so that the wick is held in place vertically.

4 Stuff the bowl with paper towels. Rest the shell on the towels, adding more towels to hold it in place. Make sure that the shell sits straight, so that when it is filled with wax, the wax will be level across the shell opening.

5 Melt the soy wax in a double boiler (see page 12) until it reaches 140°F (60°C). If necessary, stir with a wooden spoon to disperse the wax.

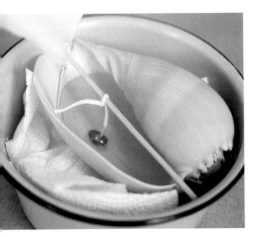

6 Pour the wax into the shell (using a pitcher/jug if your double boiler does not have a lip to pour from), stopping a little under the rim of the shell. Leave to set completely for at least two hours.

7 Slide the skewer out of the knot and untie the knot carefully.

8 Trim the wick so that it measures about ¾in (2cm). Take the shell out of the bowl.

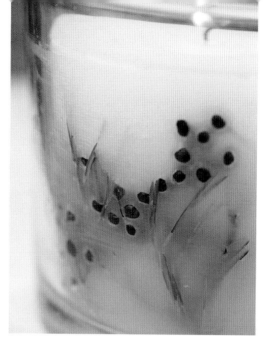

MATERIALS

Stearin

Paraffin wax (see page 12 for quantities)

Fresh fir and berries

Thick glass vase

Smaller glass jar or vase

Wick

Wick sustainer

Wax adhesive

TOOLS

Basic candle-making kit (see page 11)

Paintbrush

Small pliers

Wooden skewer

Scissors

BERRIES *and fir candle*

Fresh berries and fir are used in this frosty-looking winter candle. These are perfect placed by a front gate or door to welcome guests for a festive gathering.

1 Melt the stearin in the double boiler (see page 12). Add the paraffin wax and melt to a temperature of 180°F (80°C). If necessary, stir with a wooden spoon to disperse the wax.

2 Cut small pieces of fir and small clusters of berries. Using the paintbrush, paint a little wax inside the vase and stick the fir and berries to the inside of the vase. Don't use too much wax for this, just a few dabs to hold the plants in place.

3 Put the smaller jar or vase inside the larger one. Pour wax carefully in between the two, making sure that it does not splash. Use a pitcher (jug) if your double boiler does not have a lip to pour from. Leave to cool.

4 When the wax is hard, very carefully pour hot water into the inner jar or vase and leave for a few seconds. This will melt the wax a little so that the jar or vase can be gently twisted and lifted out.

5 Cut a length of wick the height of the vase, plus about 2in (5cm). Fix the end of it into a wick sustainer using the pliers. Using a small piece of wax adhesive, fasten the wick sustainer to the inside bottom of the vase, scraping away any excess wax to stick it in place.

6 Cut a piece of wooden skewer so that it can rest across the rim of the vase. Tie the wick onto it with a loose knot.

7 Check the temperature of the wax and heat up again if necessary to 180°F (80°C). Pour it into the vase up to the wax rim and leave to cool for about one hour.

8 The wax will dip, so heat the molten wax again in the double boiler and top up the candle so that the surface is level. Again, leave to cool completely.

9 Slide the skewer out of the knot and untie the wick, trimming it to about ¾in (2cm).

EGGSHELL *candles*

Choose eggs in shades of pale blue and green if you can get them, although plain white ones work, too. These candles would be lovely decorations for Easter, simply surround them with moss and narcissi for a pretty spring feel.

MATERIALS

Pretty colored eggs (pale green, blue, and white)

Egg box

Ready-made wicks and wick sustainers

Wax adhesive

Paper towels

Soy wax

TOOLS

Basic candle-making kit (see page 11)

Knife

Bowl

Dolly pin (clothes peg)

Scissors

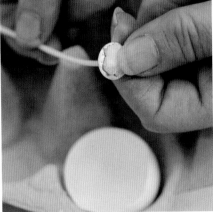

1 Crack the egg using a knife. Try to cut the egg toward the top, making sure that you create a neat crack without too many smaller cracks. Empty the egg out and wash and dry the shell carefully. Place it gently in the egg box.

2 Using a small piece of wax adhesive, stick the wick and wick sustainer into the bottom of the shell. Press it down very carefully so that the shell does not break.

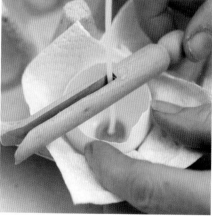

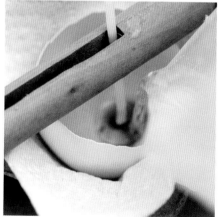

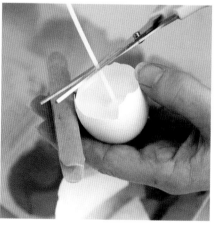

3 Put a small piece of paper towel underneath the eggshell to hold it in place. Make sure that the wick is upright inside the eggshell and hold it in place with a dolly pin (clothes peg) resting gently across the top.

4 Melt some soy wax in the double boiler (see page 12) until the temperature reaches 140°F (60°C). Tip the molten wax into the pitcher (jug) and very carefully pour it into the eggshell, aiming into the middle of the shell and trying not to splash the wax around.

5 Leave the wax to harden for a couple of hours. Remove the pin (peg) and trim the wick down to ¾in (2cm).

PRETTY COLORED CANDLES *in glass bowls*

Molded and pressed glass bowls make wonderful containers for candles. When lit, the light bounces off the glass, creating a lovely sparkling effect. I added small amounts of dye to soy wax to make delicate pastel colors.

MATERIALS

Wick

Wick sustainer

Wax adhesive

Soy wax (see page 12 for quantities)

Candle dye

TOOLS

Basic candle-making kit (see page 11)

Small pliers

Glass bowl

Scissors

Wooden skewer

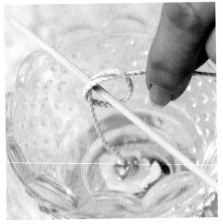

1 Cut a length of wick long enough to fit in the bowl, plus about 2in (5cm). Thread it onto a wick sustainer and fix in place with pliers.

2 Using a small piece of wax adhesive, stick the wick and sustainer to the bottom of the bowl and press down firmly to hold it in place.

3 Cut a piece of wooden skewer so that it can rest across the rim of the bowl. Tie the wick onto it with a loose knot so that the wick is held in place vertically.

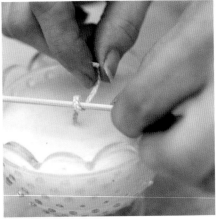

4 Heat the soy wax in the double boiler (see page 12) until it reaches 140°F (60°C). Add a tiny piece of candle dye—you will not need much at all and can always add more if you need to. Stir to disperse the color. See page 12 for tips on adding dye.

5 Pour the wax into the bowl, pouring it into the center with a slow, steady stream. Use a pitcher (jug) if your double boiler does not have a lip to pour from.

6 Leave the wax to harden for a couple of hours. Untie the knot, remove the skewer, and trim the wick down to about ¾in (2cm).

MATERIALS

Wick sustainers

Wick

Wax adhesive

Vintage tins

Soy wax

TOOLS

Basic candle-making kit (see page 11)

Small pliers

Wooden skewer

Scissors

VINTAGE TINS *with multiple wicks*

Before filling a tin with wax, pour water into it to make sure it is watertight. The tins will become very hot when lit so they are best placed on a surface that will not scorch.

1 For a long tin, cut three lengths of wick long enough to fit in the tin, plus about 2in (5cm). Using the pliers, fasten a wick sustainer to one end of each length of wick.

2 Using three small pieces of wax adhesive, stick the wicks to the bottom of the long tin, spacing them out evenly.

3 Cut a piece of wooden skewer so that it can rest across the rim of the tin. Tie the wicks to it, making sure that they are taut.

4 Melt the wax in the double boiler (see page 12) until it reaches 140°F (60°C).

5 Pour the wax into the pitcher (jug), then carefully pour it into the tin, stopping about ½in (1cm) before the rim.

6 Leave to harden completely. Slide the skewer out of the knots and trim the wicks down to about ¾in (2cm).

MATERIALS

Wooden wick and metal wick sustainer (these are usually sold together)

Wax adhesive

Rustic-looking plant pot (if your pot has a drainage hole, seal it with some mold seal)

Soy wax

TOOLS

Basic candle-making kit (see page 11)

Scissors

PLANT POT CANDLES *with wooden wicks*

Wooden wicks create a more robust-looking candle, with the added bonus that they burn with a merry crackling sound. Use plant pots with a rustic look for candles that are perfect for burning outdoors.

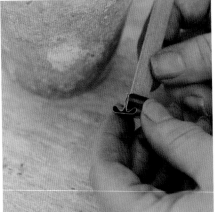

1 Push the end of the wooden wick into the metal wick sustainer so that it is vertically upright.

2 Using a small piece of wax adhesive, fix the base of the wick sustainer to the bottom of the plant pot.

3 Put the soy wax into the double boiler (see page 12) and melt it to a temperature of 140°F (60°C).

4 Pour the wax into the pitcher (jug), then pour it slowly and steadily into the plant pot, stopping about ¾in (2cm) from the top. Leave to harden for at least 24 hours.

5 Trim the wooden wick down to about ¾in (2cm).

CHAPTER 3 SCENTED *candles*

CINNAMON- AND ORANGE-SCENTED CANDLES *in enamel mugs*

Utilitarian-looking enamel mugs can create beautiful candles, and adding cinnamon and orange scents to the wax gives them a deliciously wintery feel. When the wax is molten the mugs will become hot, so make sure that you place them on a suitable surface to avoid scorch marks.

MATERIALS

Wick

Wick sustainer

Enamel mug

Wax adhesive

Soy wax

Cinnamon scent and orange scent

TOOLS

Basic candle-making kit (see page 11)

Scissors

Small pliers

Wooden skewer

Teaspoon

1 Cut a length of wick to the height of the mug, plus about 2in (5cm). Thread the end through a wick sustainer and squeeze the sustainer with pliers to fix it in place.

2 Take a small piece of wax adhesive and use it to stick the wick sustainer and wick inside the mug. Press it down firmly. Tie the end of the wick around a small piece of wooden skewer so that the wick is taut and the skewer rests on the rim of the mug.

3 Melt the soy wax in a double boiler (see page 12) and heat to 140°F (60°C). Add a few drops of orange and cinnamon scent (see page 12 for tips on using scents). Stir the scent in gently.

4 Pour the wax into the mug, pouring slowly and smoothly so that it does not splash. Leave the candle to cool completely.

5 If the wax dips in the middle (soy wax doesn't usually dip), then melt a little more wax in the same way and top up the candle. When the wax is hard, slide the skewer out and untie the wick. Trim the wick to about ¾in (2cm).

ROSE-SCENTED *flower candles*

MATERIALS

Wick

Flower-shaped rubber molds

Mold seal

Scrap cardstock

Vybar (optional) (see page 9)

Paraffin wax (make sure that it does not have added stearin as this can damage the rubber mold)

Candle dyes (I used red, pink, and black)

Rose scent

Dishwashing liquid

TOOLS

Basic candle-making kit (see page 11)

Scissors

Wicking needle

Wooden skewer

Bowl

These beautiful candles are made using rubber molds that create very intricate flower shapes—they look stunning when grouped together. They will drip wax when burning, so ensure they are on suitable bases to prevent damage.

1 Cut a length of wick about 4in (10cm) longer than the height of the rubber mold and thread the wicking needle with it. Push the needle through the middle of the top of the mold and pull about 2in (5cm) of the wick through, taking the needle off when you have finished.

2 Put a piece of mold seal around the wick on the outside of the mold to prevent any molten wax seeping through the hole.

3 Take a piece of wooden skewer and tie the other end of the wick around it so that the wick is taut.

4 Cut a circle out of the cardstock to roughly the size of the smallest part of the rubber mold. Push the mold inside it so that the cardstock becomes a collar. Rest it across a bowl so that the inside of the mold faces upward.

5 Melt the paraffin wax in the double boiler and add vybar, if using. Add small pieces of dye—see page 12 for tips on adding dyes.

6 Check the temperature of the wax and raise it to 180°F (80°C). Leave it to drop to 165°F (75°C) and add some of the rose scent (see page 12 for tips on using scents). Stir the scent in gently.

7 Carefully pour wax into the mold (using a pitcher/jug if your double boiler does not have a lip on it) until the wax reaches the top of the shaped part of the mold.

8 Pour cold water into the bowl to help cool the wax, making sure that water does not splash into the molten wax.

9 Leave the wax to harden for about an hour and if it has dipped in the middle (paraffin wax usually does), heat up a little more of the wax in the double boiler and top it up.

10 Leave for about two hours so that the wax feels hard and is just about cold (if it still feels warm leave it a little longer). Remove the wooden skewer, and trim the wick at the base of the candle. Take the mold out of the bowl, and remove the cardstock collar.

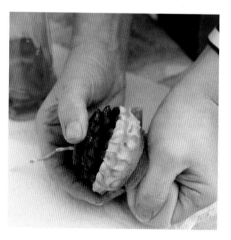

11 Remove the mold seal. To take the mold off the candle, squirt a little dishwashing liquid onto the outside of the rubber mold and using both hands, roll the mold back over itself to reveal the candle. This can be tricky but the dishwashing liquid should help to release the mold. Trim the wick to about ¾in (2cm).

LAVENDER CANDLES
in mason jars

This project is perfect if you want to make a batch of candles for gifting—mason jars can be bought in bulk from online suppliers or craft stores. For a finishing touch, tie a bow with raffia or ribbon, and add a handwritten label.

MATERIALS

Ready-made wicks and wick sustainers

Glass mason jar with lid

Wax adhesive

Soy wax

Lavender scent

Dried lavender

TOOLS

Basic candle-making kit (see page 11)

Dolly pin (clothes peg)

Scissors

1 Put a small piece of wax adhesive onto the bottom of the wick sustainer and stick it inside the jar, placing it in the center. Press down (use the end of a spoon if your hand is too large to fit in the jar).

2 Rest the dolly pin (clothes peg) across the top of the jar with the wick between the arms of the peg. This will keep the wick in place while the wax is hardening.

3 Put the soy wax into the double boiler (see page 12) and melt it until the temperature reaches 140°F (60°C). Turn off the heat and leave the temperature to drop to 130°F (55°C). Add a few drops of the lavender scent (see page 12 for tips on using scents). Stir the scent in gently.

4 Pour the wax into to the pitcher (jug) and fill the jar, stopping at the beginning of the neck of the jar.

5 Leave the wax until the surface starts to look a little opaque (this will probably take about 10 minutes). Soy wax should not dip when setting but if yours looks like it is dipping, leave it for about 20 minutes and melt more wax to top it up. Sprinkle lavender on the surface and remove the dolly pin (clothes peg). Trim the wick to about ¾in (2cm) and leave the candle to set overnight.

MATERIALS

Wick

6½lb (3kg) beeswax pellets

Citronella oil

TOOLS

Ruler

Scissors

Dipping can

Saucepan

Thermometer

Long ruler or wooden dowel
—to use as a drying rack

Scrap paper or newspaper

Sharp knife

HAND-DIPPED BEESWAX CANDLES
with citronella

When dipping, beeswax dries in thicker layers than paraffin wax, so although these candles are quite chunky, they don't take too long. Citronella oil has insect-repelling properties so these are perfect for burning outside on warm summer evenings. For indoor candles, simply omit the scent.

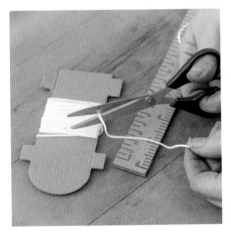

1 Measure and cut a length of wick 20in (50cm) long. Each length of wick will make two candles.

2 Put the beeswax in the dipping can and put the can in a saucepan. Half-fill the saucepan with water. Heat the water and melt the beeswax to a temperature of 140°F (60°C).

3 Take the dipping can off the heat and let the temperature drop a little. Add a few drops of citronella oil to the wax and mix it in gently.

4 Set up a drying rack for the candles: prop a ruler (or a piece of wood that is at least 1¼in/3cm wide) across two tall glass jars (or something similar) that are at least 10in (25cm) tall. Holding the wick in the middle between your thumb, index, and middle fingers (as shown in the photo), dip the ends in the wax, stopping just short of your fingers. Hold in place for no more than a couple of seconds, and in one smooth movement, pull out of the wax.

5 Hang the dipped wick on the ruler for a couple of minutes and then repeat the dipping. You can put old newspaper underneath to catch any drips. Hang to dry for another couple of minutes. Continue in the same way so that the wax builds up. If the molten wax in the dipping can becomes opaque or seems lumpy, reheat it to about 140°F (60°C), then take off the heat and continue dipping. These candles were dipped about 20 times, so continue until your candles are your desired thickness.

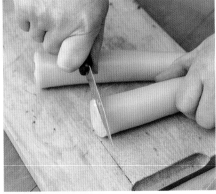

6 Using a sharp knife, slice the bottom off the candle to create a flat base. Dip one last time, then hang to dry for a few hours, or ideally overnight. Cut the wick to separate the candles, then trim each wick to about ¾in (2cm). Leave them for couple of days before burning.

MATERIALS

Pretty teacup and saucer

Ready-made wick and wick sustainer

Wax adhesive

Soy wax

Blue and red dyes

Hyacinth scent

TOOLS

Basic candle-making kit (see page 11)

Scissors

Dolly pin (clothes peg)

HYACINTH CANDLE *in a teacup*

Floral scents fit particularly well with vintage teacups and the hyacinth-scented oil used here creates a candle that smells and looks beautiful.

1 Take a small piece of wax adhesive and stick the wick and sustainer inside the cup, pressing down firmly.

2 Rest the dolly pin (clothes peg) across the rim of the cup with the wick held in the center. This will help to keep the wick in place.

3 Melt the wax in the double boiler (see page 12) and add small pieces of red and blue dyes (you won't need much), stirring gently to create a soft lilac color. See page 12 for tips on adding dye.

4 Let the wax reach 140°F (60°C), then leave to drop in temperature slightly (to about 130°F/55°C) and add the scent, stirring it in. See page 12 for tips on using scents.

5 Pour the wax into the pitcher (jug), then carefully pour the wax into the cup, being careful not to splash any.

6 Leave the wax to harden. If it dips, then melt some more wax, top it up, and leave to harden again. Remove the dolly pin (clothes peg) and trim the wick to about ¾in (2cm).

MATERIALS

Ready-made wicks and wick sustainers

Small metal tins

Wax adhesive

Soy wax

Scents (I used geranium and verbena)

TOOLS

Basic candle-making kit (see page 11)

Scissors

Dolly pin (clothes peg)

SCENTED CANDLES *in tins*

These are a prettier version of a tea light. If using them individually (or giving them as gifts) add plenty of scent so they have a strong aroma when lit, but use less if grouping the candles together so the smell will not be overwhelming.

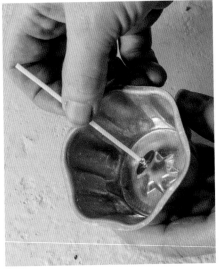

1 Take a small piece of wax adhesive and stick it to the bottom of the wick sustainer. Stick it inside the tin and press firmly to fix it in place.

2 Put the soy wax in the double boiler (see page 12) to melt. Check the temperature using the thermometer, and when it reaches 140°F (60°C), turn the heat off. Allow the wax to cool to 130°F (55°C) and add a few drops of each scent. See page 12 for tips on using scents.

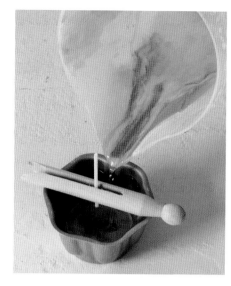

3 Rest the dolly pin (clothes peg) across the rim of the tin with the wick held in the center. This will keep the wick in place. Pour the wax into the pitcher (jug) and fill the tin, stopping a little below the rim.

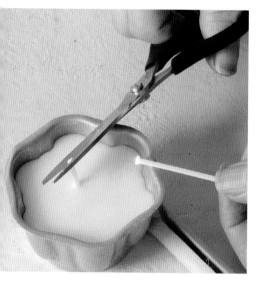

4 Leave the wax to harden for at least two hours, then remove the dolly pin (clothes peg) and trim the wick to about ¾in (2cm).

CHAPTER 4 HANDMADE *candles*

DIPPED CANDLES *in fall colors*

MATERIALS

Wick

6½lb (3kg) paraffin wax

Dyes (I used red, orange, and yellow)

TOOLS

Garden canes and two chairs—to use as a drying rack

Scrap paper or newspaper

Scissors

Ruler

12in (30cm) dipping can

Large saucepan

Wooden spoon

White plate

Thermometer

Sharp knife and cutting board

Making dipped candles can become quite addictive. Dipping the wicks over and over so that the candles grow before your eyes is a magical process and creates beautifully imperfect candles that have a real handmade charm.

1 Set up somewhere for the candles to dry before you start. Garden canes balanced across two chairs make an effective drying frame. Put old newsapaper underneath to catch any drips.

2 To make candles measuring 10in (25cm), cut some wick to a total length of 24in (60cm). Each length of wick will make two candles.

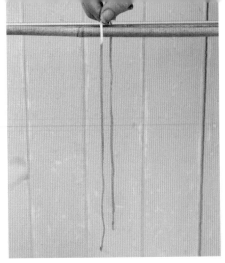

3 Put the dipping can in the saucepan, pour water into the saucepan, and heat it up. Add the paraffin wax to the dipping can and melt it, adding small pieces of dye. See page 12 for tips on adding dyes. Spoon a little wax onto a white plate and leave to dry. Although this won't show you the density of the final color, it will help you decide if more dye needs to be added.

4 Heat the wax to 180°F (80°C). Turn the heat off and leave the wax to cool to about 160°F (70°C). If it is too hot, it will melt the layers of wax already on the wick as you dip it. Holding the wick in the middle between your thumb, index, and middle fingers, dip the ends of the wick into the wax, stopping just short of your fingers. Hold in place for no more that a couple of seconds, and in one smooth movement, pull out of the wax.

5 Hang the dipped wick over the garden canes and leave for a couple of minutes to harden.

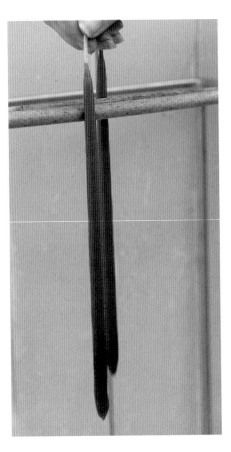

6 Continue to dip in the same way so that the wax builds up. If the molten wax in the dipping can becomes opaque or seems a little lumpy, reheat it to about 160°F (70°C), then take off the heat and continue dipping.

7 These candles were dipped about 20 times, so continue until your candles reach your desired thickness. When you have finished dipping, leave to dry on the canes for several hours, then cut the wick to separate the candles. To make a batch of different colored candles, start with a pale color of wax, make a few candles, then add more dye, and repeat.

MATERIALS

Sheets of beeswax

Wick

TOOLS

Cutting mat or scrap paper

Metal ruler

Craft knife

Scissors

Hairdryer (optional)

ROLLED BEESWAX *candles*

These beautiful candles are so easy to make, you'll never want to buy them again. Beeswax sheets can be bought from candle-making suppliers and are available in a range of colors, but I love the honey-colored sheets used here.

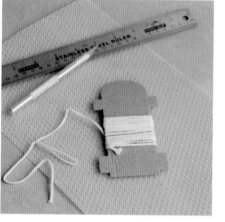

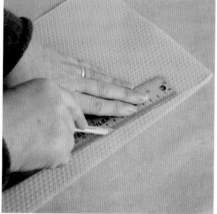

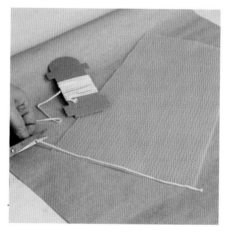

1 Lay the sheet of beeswax on the cutting mat or scrap paper. Measure 1½in (4cm) into the bottom right corner and make a small nick with your craft knife to mark it. Lay your ruler on the wax sheet from the nick to the top right corner and cut through the wax to remove a triangle from the long edge. When rolled up, this side will be the top of your candle, creating a tapered look.

2 Cut a length of wick 1¼in (3cm) longer than the height of the wax and lay it along the longer of the two side edges of the wax.

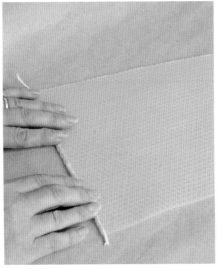

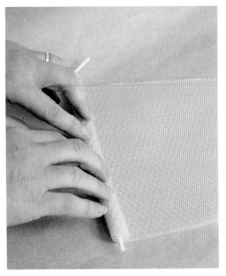

3 If your room is warm, then the wax sheet will probably be supple enough to roll, but if you are working in a cold room you may need to warm the wax sheet with a hairdryer for a few seconds to soften it slightly. Start to roll the wax sheet up over the wick, making sure that you press down slightly so that the wick is firmly held in place.

4 Continue to roll the wax up, ensuring the bottom is flat. Make sure that the roll is quite tight.

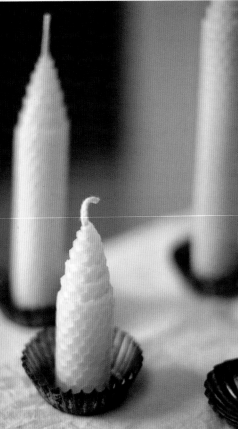

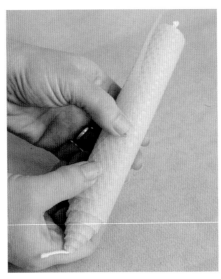

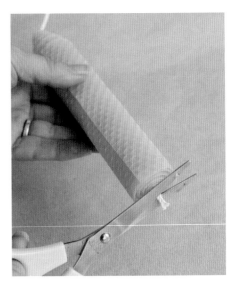

5 Gently press the edge of the sheet down with your finger to seal the wax neatly.

6 Cut the wick off the bottom of the candle, then trim the wick at the top to about ¾in (2cm).

MATERIALS

Wick

6½lb (3kg) paraffin wax

Cream dye

TOOLS

Scissors

Ruler

12in (30cm) dipping can

Large saucepan

Thermometer

Wooden spoon

Garden canes and two chairs—to use as a drying rack

Scrap paper or newspaper

Rolling pin

A twist on plain dipped candles, these charming tapers are far easier to make than they look. After making plain dipped candles, I simply twisted them from top to bottom while the wax was still warm to create unusual shapes with an elegant beauty.

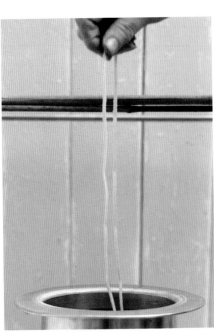

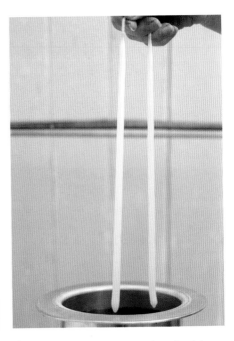

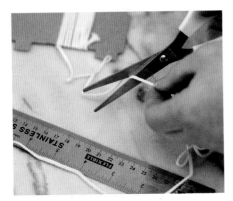

1 To make candles measuring 10in (25cm), cut some wick to a total length of 24in (60cm). Each length of wick will make two candles.

2 Put the wax into the dipping can and place into the saucepan, filling the saucepan with water. Heat up until the wax melts to a temperature of 180°F (80°C). Add a small piece of cream dye, or leave it out if you would prefer plain white candles. See page 12 for tips on adding dye. Stir gently to disperse the dye. Turn the heat off.

3 Set up somewhere for the candles to dry before you start. Garden canes balanced across two chairs make an effective drying frame. Put old newspaper underneath to catch any drips. Holding the length of wick in the middle between your thumb, index, and middle fingers, dip the wick into the molten wax, stopping just short of your fingers. Hold in place for no more than a couple of seconds, and in one smooth movement, pull out of the wax. Place over the canes to dry for a couple of minutes. If there are any kinks in the wick, simply straighten them with your fingers as the wax dries.

4 Continue to dip the wick to build up the wax. Make sure that you leave it for a couple of minutes between each dip or the wax may not have time to set between each layer. If the molten wax in the dipping can becomes opaque or seems lumpy, reheat it to 180°F (80°C).

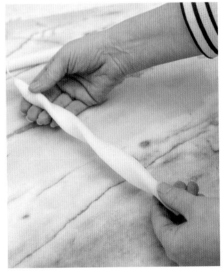

5 These candles were dipped 20 times so continue until you have your required thickness.

6 Once you've finished dipping, leave the candles to dry for two minutes, then cut the wick to separate the candles. Lay a candle on a clean, dry surface and use the rolling pin to flatten it slightly, leaving the base of the candle round.

7 Hold the top of the candle in your right hand and the base in your left hand and gently twist the candle to make even twists. Work quickly as the wax may begin to crack as it cools. Repeat with the second candle and leave to dry for several hours.

COLORED PILLAR *candles*

Plastic molds are easy to use and if you look after them, they will last a long time. Avoid using scented oils in plastic molds as they can damage the plastic.

MATERIALS

Wick

Mold seal

Stearin

Paraffin wax

Dyes (I used pink, orange, green, teal, and blue)

TOOLS

Basic candle-making kit (see page 11)

Plastic pillar candle mold

Wooden skewer

Scissors

Large glass jar

Weight (a stone or a can)

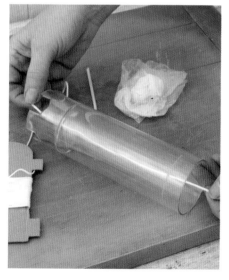

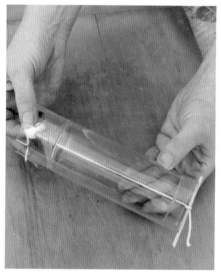

1 Thread the wick through the hole at the bottom of the mold from the outside to the inside, pull it through to the top, and tie this end of the wick onto a small piece of wooden skewer that is long enough to rest across the top of the mold.

2 Pull the end of the wick at the bottom of the mold taut and place a piece of mold seal over the hole and the wick. Cut the wick so that it is about 2½in (4cm) long. Press the mold seal firmly around the hole so it is completely sealed.

3 Put the stearin and wax into the double boiler and melt it to a temperature of 180°F (80°C). Wax at a temperature over 180°F (80°C) may crack the mold.

4 Add dye to the double boiler. See page 12 for tips on using dyes. Stir the dye through to mix it in thoroughly. Turn off the heat.

5 Pour the wax into the pitcher (jug) and carefully pour it into the mold. You can fill the mold almost to the top or use less wax if you would like a shorter candle. Save a little molten wax so that the candle can be topped up as it dries.

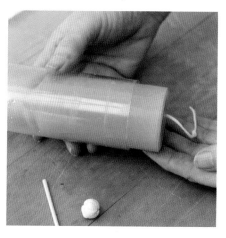

6 Put the mold carefully inside the large jar. Balance a weight on top of the mold and pour water into the jar to the level of the top of the wax. Make sure that no water drips inside the mold. This will speed up the cooling time and give a shinier finish to your candle.

7 Leave for at least an hour, by which time the wax will have dipped in the middle. Remove the mold from the jar. Re-heat the spare wax, and using the pitcher (jug) again, pour it into the mold so that the candle has a flat top (this will be the bottom of the candle when it is removed from the mold).

8 Leave the wax to set for a few hours. To remove the candle from the mold, remove the skewer from one end and take the mold seal off the other end of the mold. Turn the mold over and the candle should slip out. If the candle does not come out easily, put it in the fridge for half an hour and try again. Trim the wick at both ends of the candle, leaving the top about ¾in (2cm) long.

MATERIALS

Wick

Beeswax pellets or blocks

TOOLS

Scissors

Ruler

Clean, dry can

Saucepan

Wooden spoon

Thermometer

Wooden or metal skewer and empty plant pot—for drying candles

Heatproof gloves

Sharp knife

HAND-DIPPED
birthday candles

These tiny candles are surprisingly quick to make and add a personal touch to a birthday cake. Make them from beeswax for a subtle look or use paraffin wax and add bright dyes if your theme is more colorful.

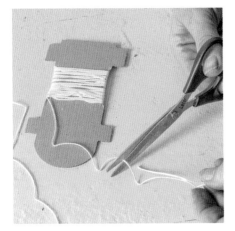

1 Cut several lengths of wick to 10in (25cm). Each length of wick will make two candles.

2 Fill the can with beeswax and put it into the saucepan. Pour water into the saucepan so that it reaches about halfway up the can. Heat the water to melt the wax, topping the wax up with more solid wax so that it is full of molten wax. When the temperature reaches 140°F (60°C), turn the heat off. Wearing heatproof gloves, remove the can carefully from the saucepan, taking care not to spill the wax. Place the can on a cutting board.

3 Set up a drying rack by balancing a skewer across an empty pot (it needs to be at least 6in/15cm tall). Holding a length of cut wick in the middle between your thumb and index finger, dip the ends of the wick into the wax, stopping just short of your fingers. Hold in place for no more than a couple of seconds, and in one smooth movement, pull out of the wax.

4 If there are any kinks in the wick, simply straighten them with your fingers as the wax dries. Hang the wick over the skewer for a couple of minutes. Dip the wicks in the wax again and hang to dry for another couple of minutes.

5 Dip the wicks in the wax about five times in total, leaving them to dry between each dip. The bottoms of the candles will become a little misshapen, so when you've finished dipping, cut the bottoms of the candles off with a sharp knife to straighten them. Leave to dry overnight, then cut the wicks to separate the candles. Trim the wicks to ½in (1cm).

BLOCK *candles*

These contemporary-looking block candles are made in juice cartons that are very easy to remove because they can simply be ripped off. The inside of the cartons gives the candles an attractive matt finish.

MATERIALS

Empty drink carton

Thick cardstock

Tape

Wick

Wick sustainer

Wax adhesive

Paraffin wax

Dyes (I used pink, purple, and gray)

TOOLS

Basic candle-making kit (see page 11)

Scissors

Small pliers

Wooden skewer

1 Using scissors, cut off the top of the drink carton. Wash and dry the inside of the carton. Fold the cardstock around the carton and tape it in place. This will prevent the sides of the carton from bowing and will help to keep the candle square.

2 Cut the wick so that it measures the height of the carton, plus about 2in (5cm). Fasten a wick sustainer to one end of it using the small pliers. Take a small piece of wax adhesive and use it to stick the wick sustainer and wick inside the bottom of the carton.

3 Cut a piece of wooden skewer slightly longer than the width of the carton and rest it across the top. Tie the wick to it so that it is held taut.

4 Melt the wax in the double boiler until it reaches 180°F (80°C).

5 Add small pieces of dye and stir it through the wax to mix it in.

6 Pour the wax into the pitcher (jug) and pour it into the carton to your required height.

7 After about an hour, check the candle and if it has dipped (paraffin wax tends to do so), reheat the remaining wax and top it up to create a flat top.

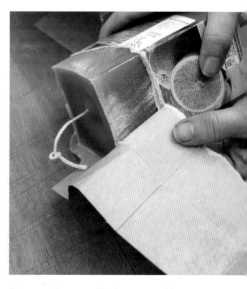

8 Leave the candle for several hours, then remove the wooden skewer. Carefully rip the carton off to reveal the candle. Trim the wick to about ¾in (2cm).

MATERIALS

White candles (use store-bought or make your own—see page 78)

Marbling paints suitable for candles

TOOLS

Plastic bag

Large bucket (make sure this is as deep as the height of your candles)

Pitcher (jug)

Newspaper

Protective gloves

Wooden skewer

Paper towels

Candle holder

MARBLED *candles*

These beautiful candles are really easy to make. Marbling paints are available online and from craft stores, but make sure they are suitable for use on candles before buying.

1 If you're making your own candles, follow Steps 1–5 on pages 78–80, omitting the dye. Open the plastic bag and place it in the bucket, pulling it over the rim of the bucket. This will keep the bucket clean.

2 Fill the bag with cold water, stopping just short of the top. Cover your work surface with newspaper. It is also a good idea to have a garbage bag to hand as well.

3 Wearing protective gloves, take the black paint and shake the bottle. Remove the lid and drip a few drops of paint onto the surface of the water.

4 Shake the bottle of white paint and add some drops of this onto the surface of the water.

5 Using the wooden skewer, gently swirl the paints together. Mixing them a lot will give a finer marbling pattern, but you can experiment with this if you are marbling several candles.

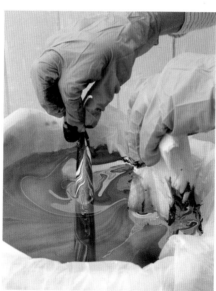

6 Hold a piece of paper towel in one hand and the candle in your other hand, holding the wick between your thumb and index finger. Dip the candle into the bucket and hold in place for a few seconds.

7 Still holding the candle underwater, wipe the paper towel over the surface of the water to remove the paint. If you do not do this, the candle will get another coat of paint and the pattern will not be well-defined.

8 Take the candle out of the water. Hold it over the bucket for about 30 seconds to dry a little, then put into a candle holder to dry completely. Wipe another piece of paper towel over the surface of the water to remove any remaining streaks of paint. Continue to marble more candles in the same way, ensuring that the surface of the water is clean between each one. Leave the candles to dry overnight before lighting.

CHAPTER 5 USING molds

COLORFUL *teardrop candles*

MATERIALS

Wick

Mold seal

Scrap cardstock

Large glass jar

Vybar (optional) (see page 9)

Paraffin wax (make sure that it does not have added stearin as this can damage the rubber mold)

Dyes (I used yellow, pink, orange, and red)

Dishwashing liquid

TOOLS

Basic candle-making kit (see page 11)

Scissors

Wick needle

Rubber mold

Wooden skewer

Rubber molds are available in a wide range of shapes—these teardrop candles are made with molds in three different sizes using paraffin wax in citrus colors. The molds can be tricky to remove, but using a little dishwashing liquid helps to prevent damage so they can be used multiple times.

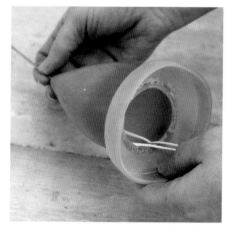

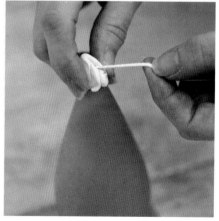

1 Cut a length of wick about 4in (10cm) longer than the height of the rubber mold and thread the wicking needle with it. Push the needle through the center of the top of the mold and pull a few inches (centimeters) through, taking the needle off.

2 Put a piece of mold seal around the wick on the outside of the mold to prevent any molten wax seeping through the hole.

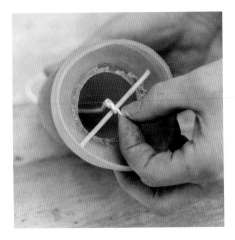

3 Take a piece of wooden skewer and tie the bottom end of the wick around it so that the wick is held taut.

4 Cut a circle out of the cardstock about the size of the bottom part of the rubber mold (as shown in the photo above), push the mold inside it so that the cardstock circle becomes a collar and rest it across the glass jar so that the inside of the mold faces upward.

5 Melt the paraffin wax in the double boiler and add vybar, if using. Add small pieces of dye—see page 12 for tips on adding dyes.

6 Raise the temperature of the wax to 180°F (80°C). Using a pitcher (jug), carefully pour wax into the mold until the wax reaches the top of the shaped part of the mold.

7 Pour cold water into the jar to help cool the wax, making sure that water does not splash into the molten wax.

8 Leave the wax to harden for about an hour, and if it has dipped in the middle (paraffin wax usually does), heat up a little more of the wax in the double boiler and top it up.

9 Leave for a couple of hours so that the wax feels hard and is just about cold (if it still feels warm, leave it a little longer). Remove the wooden skewer, trim the wick at the bottom of the candle, and take the mold out of the jar. Remove the cardstock collar.

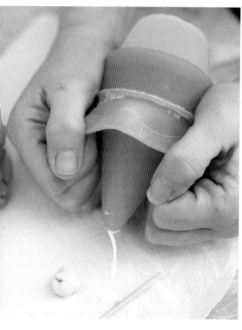

10 Take the mold seal off, squirt a little dishwashing liquid onto the outside of the rubber mold, and using both hands, roll the mold back over itself to reveal the candle. This can be tricky but the dishwashing liquid should help to release the mold. Trim the wick to about ¾in (2cm).

MATERIALS

¾oz (20g) stearin

2½oz (70g) soy wax

7oz (200g) paraffin wax

Ready-made wicks and wick sustainers measuring 4in (10cm)

TOOLS

Basic candle-making kit (see page 11)

3 metal brioche molds measuring 2¾in (7cm), 3in (7.5cm), and 4in (10cm) in diameter

Cup

Metal awl

Paintbrush

Scissors

BRIOCHE MOLD *trees*

Metal brioche pans with lovely fluted edges make ideal molds for candles. Using three different-sized molds creates a tiered effect to make these adorable trees —perfect for festive decorations. White wax has a simple, classic look and arranging them on a silver tray that reflects the light creates a pretty twinkling display.

1 Melt the stearin in the double boiler, then add the soy wax and paraffin wax and allow to melt. Raise the temperature to about 160°F (70°C).

2 Transfer the molten wax to a pitcher (jug). Pour the wax into the brioche molds very carefully in a thin stream so that it does not splash. Leave the wax to harden for about an hour.

3 Reheat the wax and top up the molds if the wax has dipped (paraffin wax usually does) so that the surface is flat. Leave to set completely for a couple of hours.

4 Take the wax shapes out of the molds (they will come out easily so be careful they do not fall out and chip when you turn them over). Fill the cup with hot water. Dip the pointed end of the awl into the hot water, then make a hole in the middle of each wax shape. You may need to redip the awl in hot water between each one. Gently push the point through the wax, twisting it a little to get it through.

5 Take the largest wax shape, and from the flat underside, push the wick through the hole so that the sustainer sits flat at the bottom.

6 Thread the middle-sized wax shape onto the wick and working quickly, dab some molten wax between the two wax shapes and push the top one down onto the bottom one, pressing down firmly for a few seconds to join them. If they are not stuck together, repeat the process.

7 Thread the wick through the smallest wax shape and join it to the middle one with molten wax, as before. Dab a little wax around the top of the wick to fill in any gaps.

8 Trim the wick so that it measures about ¾in (2cm).

MATERIALS

Sand (natural colors are best)

Paraffin wax

Dyes (I used pink, orange, and yellow)

Wicks that have been dipped in wax

TOOLS

Bucket

Shaped glass tumbler

Metal spoon

Paintbrush

SAND *candles*

Sand candles are a brilliant way of creating candles without needing to buy a mold. Simply push a glass or small vase into damp sand to make a mold and fill with molten wax to create textured candles in pastel colors.

1 Put the sand in the bucket or tub and compress it with the palms of your hand to get rid of any air pockets. Wet the sand if it is too dry. Scoop a little sand away and plunge the glass tumbler into the bucket. Using a metal spoon, neatly flatten the sand around the rim of the glass.

2 Press your fingers against the inside of the tumbler and pull it out of the sand, making sure that you do not disturb the sand.

3 Put the wax into the double boiler and melt it to 180°F (80°C). Add small pieces of dye, keeping the color quite pale (see page 12), and stir gently to mix.

4 Pour the wax into the pitcher (jug) and holding the spoon upside down, pour the wax into the tumbler mold over the spoon to soften the stream of wax slightly. Fill to just short of the rim.

5 Leave the wax to form a slight opaque surface, then gently push the wick into the center and all the way down into it so it hits the bottom. It should stand upright on its own.

6 Leave the candle for an hour and then top it up with more melted wax to form a flat surface. Leave to set for a couple of hours (any longer than this and it will become harder to remove the sand from the outside of the candle), then scrape the sand away and lift the candle out of the sand.

7 Brush the surface with the paintbrush to remove loose sand. Trim the wick so that it measures about ¾in (2cm). Leave for at least 24 hours before burning the candle.

MATERIALS

Paraffin wax

Stearin

Pink and red dyes

Ready-made wicks and wick sustainers

TOOLS

Basic candle-making kit (see page 11)

Heart-shaped molds

Bradawl

Scissors

FLOATING HEART *candles*

To make several hearts in different shades of pink, multiply the amount of wax needed for one heart by the number of candles you want to make and melt all of it. Add a small amount of dye, make a few candles, then reheat the wax, add more dye to strengthen the color, and continue in the same way to create different pinks.

1 Put the wax and stearin into the double boiler and melt to a temperature of 180°F (80°C).

2 Add small pieces of dye and stir gently. If you are making several candles in different shades of pink and red, add just a small amount initially so that you start with the palest color. See the introduction above and page 12 for tips on adding dye. Make sure that the dye is well-mixed.

3 Pour the wax into a pitcher (jug) and carefully pour the wax into the mold. Leave the candle for half an hour. If the wax has dipped, top it up with a little more melted wax.

4 Leave the wax in the mold for at least an hour, then take it out of the mold. It should come out easily so make sure it doesn't fall out and break. Dip the awl into hot water for a few seconds to warm it up, then very gently push it through the wax to make a hole in the center. Twist it gently and it should go through the wax easily.

5 Thread the wick through the hole from the back to the front and push the wick sustainer into the wax slightly so that it is held in place.

6 Trim the wick so that it measures about ¾in (2cm). Leave for at least 24 hours before burning the candles. When you're ready to light the candles, float them in a bowl or dish filled with water and flowerheads, if you wish.

MATERIALS

Parchment (greaseproof) paper

16oz (450g) paraffin wax

1½oz (45g) stearin

Ready-made wick and wick sustainer

TOOLS

Basic candle-making kit (see page 11)

Square sheet pan (baking tray) with a rim measuring 12 x 12in (30 x 30cm)

4 square cookie cutters in different sizes

Cup

Metal awl

TOWER *of wax squares*

This stylish candle is made from a sheet of wax cut into squares using cookie cutters. It's important to cut the wax before it becomes too hard or it may crack.

1 Put a piece of parchment (greaseproof) paper on to the sheet pan (baking tray) and crease it along the bottom edge all the way around so that the paper sits inside the rim.

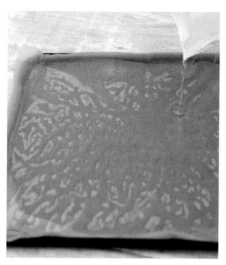

2 Heat the wax and the stearin in the double boiler until it reaches 180°F (80°C).

3 Set the tray somewhere flat and level and carefully pour the wax onto the parchment paper so that there is an even layer.

4 Leave to set for no more than 30 minutes, then using the cookie cutters cut out four wax squares in each size. If the wax is still soft, leave it for another five minutes and try again. Do not let it get too hard or it may crack when you try to cut into it.

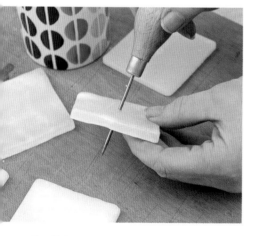

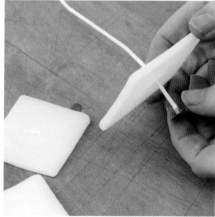

5 Fill the cup with hot water. Dip the pointed end of the awl into the hot water, then make a hole in the middle of each wax square. You may need to redip the awl in hot water between each one. Gently push the point through the wax, twisting it a little to get it through.

6 Push the wick through one of the largest squares from the underside to the top, making sure that the wick sustainer sits flat at the bottom.

7 Continue to push the wax squares on to the wick from largest to smallest. Dab a little wax around the last hole and the wick to hold it in place. Leave for at least 24 hours before burning the candle.

WAX *lanterns*

These beautiful wax lanterns will bring atmosphere to any gathering. Specialist candle-making suppliers sell paraffin wax that is labeled as having a high melting point. If you can source it, this wax would be useful for these lanterns so that they will not melt when a lit tea light is placed inside. Alternatively, use battery-powered tea lights.

MATERIALS

Paraffin wax

Cream dye

Rice or sand

TOOLS

Basic candle-making kit (see page 11)

Balloon (look for balloons that are suitable for helium as they will be thicker)

Baking dish lined with parchment (greaseproof) paper

Sharp scissors

Tea lights (candles or LED)

1 Pull the balloon onto the end of the faucet (tap) and slowly fill with tepid water. The balloon should be smaller than the size of the double boiler you are using. Take the balloon off the faucet (tap) and tie in a secure knot. Dry it thoroughly with a clean cloth.

2 Put paraffin wax in the double boiler and melt enough so that it is at least 3in (8cm) deep.

3 Add a small piece of cream dye. Check the temperature, and when it reaches 180°F (80°C) take it off the heat.

4 Line a baking dish with a piece of parchment (greaseproof) paper. Holding the knot of the filled balloon, dip the balloon into the wax about three-quarters of the way up. If your balloon has air in it, make sure that the wax does not touch the part of the balloon without water in it as it may burst.

5 Hold the balloon above the wax for a few seconds, then dip it again. Continue to dip about five more times, waiting a few seconds between each dip. Rest the balloon on the parchment paper for a minute, then continue to dip so that in total the balloon has been dipped about 15–18 times.

6 Put the balloon on the parchment paper and leave for 15 minutes to harden.

7 Hold the wax and balloon over the sink and make a small nick in the balloon on its underside (if you make a hole in the top prepare to get very wet!) and let the water drain out. The balloon should come away from the wax so it can be removed easily.

8 Remove the parchment paper from the baking dish. Put the empty dish in a hot oven for a few minutes, then take it out. Hold the lantern upside down and put the rim of it on the baking dish. Hold for a few seconds, then twist slightly and lift it off. This will make a nice, neat rim on the lantern. Leave for at least 24 hours before using the lantern.

CHAPTER 6 DECORATING
the surface

MATERIALS

Pillar candles (see page 81 for how to make them) in dark colors

Water-based size

Gold leaf sheets (about 3 per candle, depending on the size of the gold band)

TOOLS

Fine-grade sandpaper

Paintbrush

GOLD-LEAF *candles*

Add a shimmering touch to plain pillar candles with delicate gold leaf. Available from good art stores and craft suppliers, it can often be bought in a range of metallic shades and is used with adhesive called gold size. Use a water-based size, as it's easier to use and has fewer chemicals in it.

1 Take a small piece of sandpaper and very gently sand a band around the bottom of the candle. The idea is to just rough up the surface of the wax so go carefully or you may end up with wax that is too scratched.

2 Paint the sanded part of the candle with size and leave it to one side for about 10 minutes or until it has dried a little but is still tacky.

3 Take a sheet of gold leaf (on its backing paper) and press it against the glued area with the gold shiny side against the glue. Gently press down.

4 Smooth the gold leaf paper over with your fingertip to make sure that it has adhered to the candle.

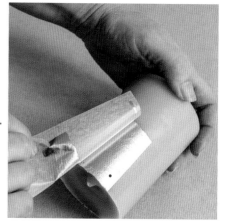

5 Peel the backing paper off gently. If any areas are not covered in gold leaf, re-apply the paper and rub again. Continue in the same way to cover the glued area. After removing the backing paper, very gently rub over the gold leaf with a dry paintbrush to remove any loose bits.

BIRCH-COVERED *candles*

Homemade or store-bought candles can be transformed with pieces of silver birch bark. Wrapped around plain pillar candles, the bark adds a touch of sophistication and a rustic twist.

MATERIALS

Paper

White pillar candle (see page 81 to make your own)

Sheet of silver birch bark (available from florists suppliers and online craft stores)

Water-based fast drying glue

String

TOOLS

Pencil

Scissors

1 Wrap the paper around the candle and mark the overlap and height of the candle onto it. Cut out a rectangle of paper to use as a template, adding ¾in (2cm) to the overlap.

2 Hold the paper template against the bark and cut out the rectangle using scissors. It should be easy to cut.

3 If the bark you are using is quite stiff, soak it in hot water for about 10 minutes. This will help to make it more flexible. Remove it from the water and dry with paper towel.

4 Wrap the bark rectangle around the candle and apply glue onto one end of it in a strip about ¾in (2cm) wide.

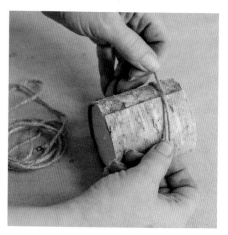

4 Press the ends of the bark down on to each other and tightly bind it with two or three lengths of string around the candle. Leave in place until the glue is completely dry, preferably overnight. Cut the string off.

CARVED *candles*

Store-bought colored candles are often plain white candles that have been over-dipped in colored wax. These are perfect for this project as carving into the colored layers of wax reveals the white underneath.

MATERIALS

Pillar candle (use ready-made colored candles with white centers, or use a plain white candle if you are going to color it yourself—see Step 1)

TOOLS

Newspaper

Lino-cutting tool

Soft paintbrush

1 If you are dipping white candles to color them, follow the steps for Dip-Dyed Candles on page 124. Dip the candles completely in colored wax (making sure that the wax is strongly colored with dye) twice and leave to dry completely.

2 Protect your work surface with newspaper. Take the lino-cutting tool in one hand, and holding the candle in your other hand, cut a wavy line from the bottom to the top of the candle. Always work with the tool pointing away from your body, as the tip is sharp.

3 Cut smaller curved lines into the wax, making sure that the lines do not join up with each other or the wax may chip off in pieces.

4 Continue to cut into the wax to make a pattern around the candle, wiping the small curls of wax away with your finger as you cut so that you can see the pattern clearly.

5 When the whole candle has been carved, brush it all over with the paintbrush to remove any flakes of wax. If any bits of wax do chip off the candle, you can heat up a spoon in hot water, dry it, press it against the candle to soften the wax, and quickly stick the chip back in place.

DIP-DYED *candles*

Brighten up plain candles with a coating of colored wax. Start with a pale color of wax, then after dipping the first candle, add more dye and continue dipping. Make the second dip lower than the first to create an ombré effect.

MATERIALS

3¼lb (1½kg) paraffin wax

Dyes (I used blue and green)

White candles (see page 72 to make your own)

TOOLS

Dipping can

Saucepan

Thermometer

Wooden spoon

Chairs—to use as drying racks

Newspaper

Scissors

1 Put the wax in the dipping can and put that in the saucepan. Fill the saucepan with hot water and melt the wax to a temperature of 180°F (80°C).

2 Add a piece of green dye and mix gently until it has melted. See page 12 for tips on adding dye. Get a few chairs ready to use as drying racks, with newspaper below to catch any drips.

3 Take the dipping can off the heat. Take two of the candles (if they are joined together; if not, dip them individually) and dip one of them about halfway.

4 Hold it for a few seconds, then dip it again holding it slightly higher in the dipping can than the first dip so that the color will graduate slightly. Hang the candle up on the chair and leave for a few minutes so that the wax sets.

5 Return the dipping can to the heat and add some more green dye. Mix again, then dip the second candle in the same way as before. The color should be slightly stronger. Leave the candles to dry.

6 Repeat this process, adding more dye as you go to make more intense colors and dipping more candles. Add some blue dye to create turquoise shades, then stronger blues. Leave all the candles to dry for several hours. Cut the wick to separate the candles and trim each wick to about ¾in (2cm).

Suppliers

NORTH AMERICA

Candle Science
www.candlescience.com
Useful general candle-making supplier

Candlewic
3765 Old Easton Road
Doylestown, PA 18902
800-368-3352
www.candlewic.com
Everything you need for candle-making,
in-store and online

The Flaming Candle
www.theflamingcandle.com
Particularly good selection of scents
and oils

Jo-Ann
www.joann.com

Michaels
www.michaels.com

UK

Candle Makers Supplies
102-104 Shepherds Bush Road
London W6 7PD
020 7602 1812
www.candlemakers.co.uk
Everything you need for candle-making,
available in-store and online

L. Cornelissen & Son
105 Great Russell Street
London WC1B 3RY
020 7636 1045
www.cornelissen.com
Beautiful art shop selling gold-leaf in
a range of shades and lino-cutting tool
kits for candle carving

Flying Tiger
www.uk.flyingtiger.com
Great for plain candles to decorate
and embellish

Great Art
08433 571 572
www.greatart.co.uk
Art suppliers selling a range of marbling
paints suitable for candles

Hobbycraft
0330 026 1400
www.hobbycraft.co.uk
Large craft stores selling waxes, wicks,
and candle molds

Ikea
www.ikea.com
Great for plain candles to color-dip
or decorate

LiveMoor
01752 695 220
www.livemoor.co.uk
A wide range of waxes and fragrances
suitable for candle-making

Online Shells
01889 580668
www.onlineshells.co.uk
Stockist of beautiful shells—especially
good for large shells

The Soap Kitchen
01237 420 872
www.thesoapkitchen.co.uk
Everything you need for candle-making
as well as a wide selection of fragrances

Supplies For Candles
01709 588 579
www.suppliesforcandles.co.uk
A complete range of candle-making
materials

Index

Acknowledgments

Huge and many thanks to Debbie Patterson for such beautiful photography—as ever—and for her unstinting humor, inspiration, and enthusiasm. Thank you to Rebecca Mays for the kind loan of candlesticks. Thank you to Emily Bowling for generously supplying sage leaves for the smudge sticks. Thank you to Anna Galkina for the thoughtful editing and support throughout the project. Thank you to Gurjant Mandair for organizing locations. Thank you to Sally Powell for designing the book so beautifully. And of course, thank you to Cindy Richards for offering me the opportunity to try a new project. I am very grateful to have been able to work with a lovely team on such a fun project. Last but not least, thank you to Laurie, Gracie, and Betty—for all the things.